Shadows

A Play

Josephine Carter

Samuel French – London
New York – Sydney – Toronto – Hollywood

CHARACTERS

Erica Strong
Susan Peak, her daughter
Anne Strong, Erica's daughter
Martin Strong, Erica's son
Man
Woman
Dr Blake

The action takes place in the dining-room of a large house

Time—the present

NOTE ON THE CHARACTERS

Erica is aged between seventy and eighty. Her daughter Susan is fortyish, Anne is five years younger than Susan, and Martin five years younger than Anne. The Man and Woman are dressed simply but anonymously. Dr Blake can be male or female.

Throughout the play the Man and Woman do not "see" Susan, Anne or Martin and vice versa.

SHADOWS*

The dining room of a large house. Daytime

The room is crowded with furniture and possessions. Erica now lives solely in this room and is thus surrounded by her things. The edges of the room should be in shadow so that the Man and the Woman can merge into the background. The Man and Woman are on stage at the beginning of the play but hidden by the shadows

As the Curtain *rises Erica is dozing in a chair. The door to the room is just closing. Erica wakes*

Erica What's that. Hallo. Who's there? Where are you?

The Man comes in from the shadows

Man I'm here. Are you all right?
Erica Oh, it's you. I thought it was someone else.
Man It's probably Susan.
Erica Susan? My daughter?
Man Your daughter.

The Woman comes in from the shadows and stands by Erica

Woman Hallo, Erica. How are you?
Erica Oh, that Susan. I'm quite all right. Don't hover—go away, both of you,
Woman I, that is we, thought you might like to talk for a while.
Erica Not at the moment, thank you. I don't feel like talking to you now. I am going to make myself a cup of tea.

Erica exits to the kitchen

Woman I worry about her.
Man She's all right. Just watch, that's what we were told.

Susan is heard calling, off

Susan (*off*) Mother! Mother!

Susan enters, followed by Anne and Martin

The Man and the Woman step back into the shadows

Susan Mother, where are you?
Martin Honestly, this place is a pigsty—she shouldn't be living here.
Anne We know that—that is why we're here, just in case you have forgotten. I doubt whether we shall persuade Mother though.
Susan Don't be so defeatist. Ssh—here she comes.

Erica enters with her tea

Erica Hallo, Susan. Oh, Anne and Martin as well, what a nice surprise. (*Whispering*) I knew you had come but they said not.
Susan Who did?
Erica Did what?
Susan Who said we hadn't come?
Erica Oh ... well ... (*She gestures vaguely*) They seem to have gone. How glad I am to see you all—it's been a long time since I've seen you. (*She sits down in her chair*)
Anne I was here last week.
Erica I meant all together.
Susan Well ... we have been talking things over and we decided we should come down and talk to you.
Erica "We decided"—oh dear, that sounds ominous. Are you going to bully me, Susan?
Martin No one is going to bully you, Mother, but we must have a family discussion.
Erica Don't want to.
Anne Don't be childish, Mother.
Erica I'm not.
Susan Drink your tea before it gets cold.

Susan draws Anne and Martin to one side

Now we must tread carefully, we won't get anywhere if she gets mulish.
Anne I suppose you're blaming me again.
Susan I'm not placing any blame. Don't pick a quarrel, Anne. All I'm saying is that we must stay calm. I suggest Martin speaks to

her. After all he is the only son, the man of the house, the light of
her life.

Anne Go on then, Mummy's pet.

Martin Oh, shut up!

Anne Sorry. Susan's right. Both of us have started off on the
wrong foot. Go on.

Martin OK. OK.

Martin moves over to Erica

Well, how have you been keeping, Mother?

Erica I'm all right, dear, It's been a long time since you've been to
see me—where have you been hiding yourself?

Martin I know, I'm sorry. It's ... it's not always easy to ... But
are you well? You are looking a little peaky. Have you seen the
doctor recently?

Erica Peaky! That's not me—that's Susan, peaky by name and
peaky by nature—that's Susan.

Susan Mother! Not that old joke.

Erica Fancy becoming a Peak—from Strong to peaky, what a
come down.

Susan On the contrary—being strong I climbed to the peak.

Erica That's a new one—you've been saving that.

Susan I've had plenty of time to think about it.

Anne Will you both stop this silly argument about names.

Susan It's Mother, she always starts it. I don't know why. She was
always fond of Ted and he was, is, very fond of her.

Erica Ted? Oh yes, Ted. That's someone else I haven't seen for
ages. Where have you been hiding him? Why doesn't he come
and see me?

Susan He's in America.

Erica Why?

Susan He lives there. I've told you before.

Erica Lives there, does he. Left you, has he? Just like Sam.

Anne Sam? Who's Sam?

Martin Don't ask—we're getting right off the track.

Erica You are Sam—Susan, Anne and Martin—you are Sam.

Susan But we haven't left you, Mother—we're here.

Anne She is quite definitely batty—we must get her into a ... well
somewhere.

Erica Batty! I heard that. Don't you believe it.

Erica waves towards the Man and the Woman in the shadows. The Man moves in from the shadows

Did you hear that? They say I'm batty. Do you think I'm batty?
Man Of course not, Erica.

Erica waves the Man away. The Man moves back into the shadows

Erica You heard that, didn't you. I'm not batty—the expert says I'm not batty.
Martin Expert?
Anne I'm sorry, Mother—a slip of the tongue. I didn't know—didn't realise that you thought of us as one being—a conglomerate child as it were.
Martin A corporation. "The Sam Strong Corporation"—purveyors of dreams.
Anne Manufacturers of Fantasy.

Martin and Anne giggle

Erica Children, children, stop it. Of course I don't think of you as one child. You are all very different, and very dear, to me. Susan, always so neat, tidy and reliable. Anne, the tomboy, although who would think it to see you now and then my baby, Martin. Such a pretty boy. And so talented. What happened to all that talent Martin?
Anne We seem to have wandered off course.
Susan That, I think, was the intention.
Martin Let's forget about Sam.
Erica Sam was your father.

There is a pause

Martin Father? But father's name was Hubert.
Erica I know, but I always called him Sam. Didn't I ever tell you? No, I suppose one is reluctant to admit your disappointments and mistakes to your children.
Susan Disappointments?
Erica Yes. I can with all honesty say your father was an acute disappointment to me.
Anne And a mistake?
Erica Yes.
Martin Now she tells us! But why? I mean how . . . or do I mean why . . .?

Erica Why did I marry him? He looked so good and reliable. So different from my own family—father so strict and humourless and mother, blonde and fretful. He seemed to live up to his name, solid and strong. He looked like a Sam. I told him so, he didn't demur, until we were married and then he insisted on being called Hubert. Hubert! Looks were deceivers ever.

Martin I would have thought Hubert would have suited him.

Erica Ah, but you didn't know him when he was young.

Susan I remember him. Yes, it's a good description—solid and strong.

Anne But he had a weakness.

Erica He thought Hubert sounded more "classy". He had such a thing about class. Always wanted to be better than his neighbour. Why? I never understood it. He had a good job. A travelling salesman—went all over the country, and what was wrong with that, I'd like to know.

Martin What do you mean, Anne, he had a weakness?

Anne Need you ask? I think I knew long before mother. When he came home he'd swing me up in the air. He always smelled so sweet and that was long before the days of after shave, and mother never wore perfume. Even then, what was I? Five I suppose, even then I never said a word—some instinct told me that I didn't want to know.

Martin So it wasn't just the dancer.

Anne No—it wasn't just the dancer, she was just the one that caught him.

Erica But I tricked him. Him and his airs—thought he was marrying into class he did, marrying me. But with my parents it was all a façade, a fantasy. I tricked him, with you three I had my Sam. I don't think he ever realised. A bit simple he was—simple, solid and strong.

They all laugh

Martin But didn't you want to re-name us? I mean, after he ran off with the dancer.

Erica She ran off with Hubert. Sam stayed here (*She puts her hand on her heart*) and here (*She gestures to the three of them*)

The Woman comes in from the shadows

Woman You're signalling. Do you want something? A talk about the old days?

Erica No, no. Not to you, not now. Anyway I wasn't signalling, I was enfolding my family to my bosom. Go away.

The Woman goes back to the shadows

Susan Oh, Mother, I do love you. We all love you, but we do so worry about you. That is why we have all come together today, to try and persuade you to leave—to go into a home where you will be looked after—where you will have company.

Erica This is my home. And I have company—my shadows. I told Dr Blake that—he keeps on and on about me moving. But with my shadows I shall be safe.

Susan Mother, listen, listen carefully.. I am telling you the truth. Your "shadows" cannot keep you safe—they cannot help you and if you are in trouble, they can only talk to you.

Erica The art of conversation, what more does one need?

Martin Mother—listen to her.

Erica Later, at dinner. We'll have dinner by candlelight. Candlelight and conversation, long into the night, I should like that, I haven't been sleeping well lately.

Anne Mother!

Susan Leave it for a while, she's determined not to hear.

Martin Where do you sleep? I looked round the house, none of the other rooms seem habitable.

Erica In here. I sleep on the settee. It's quite comfortable, I've a primus stove and a sink in the old pantry there and a bathroom off.

Susan Mother, it's not a bathroom, it's just a loo. Where do you wash?

Erica In the sink.

Anne And what about a bath? Spritely as you are, Mother dear, I can hardly see you leaping into the sink.

Erica Don't need a bath, a good wash down is all I need. I don't smell. (*Shouting*) I don't smell do I?

Man (*from the shadows*) Of course not, Erica.

Susan No-one is suggesting you do. It's just that it is so unhygienic and uncomfortable.

Erica Rubbish, I am perfectly comfortable. And I keep nice and warm, snug as a bug in a rug.

Martin I don't doubt there's more truth in that than meets the eye.

Erica Do you remember that, children? Always tucked you into bed "snug as a bug in a rug".

Martin I remember. And I remember going through the rugs and carpets with a fine toothcomb, but couldn't find a thing.

Erica I'm pleased to hear it.

Anne Until that Christmas. Do you remember, Martin? We woke on Christmas morning and it was freezing. We thought it was terrible that everything should be out in the cold.

Martin Oh, yes. We went and collected every beetle, wood louse and spider we could find and brought them all in and deposited them on the rug in front of the fire.

Susan I remember. Father was furious.

Erica Oh, yes. Haughty Hubert got on his high horse that year. We didn't see much of Sam that Christmas. Do you remember . . .

Susan Now stop trying to side track us, Mother. We must talk seriously, and you can take that look off your face, you know why we are here. You must listen to reason. You just cannot live here alone any more.

Erica I am not alone, I have my sha . . .

Susan Your shadows cannot help you. You know that. Now, we cannot stay here for ever. We have . . . we have other things to do and arrangements must be made.

Erica I don't need any arrangements made.

Anne What happens if you fall?

Erica I'd pick myself up.

Martin Or if you're ill?

Erica I'd ring the doctor. The telephone is still connected—I'm not a fool you know.

Susan What if there was a fire?

There is a pause

Erica We'll talk about it over dinner. We'll have dinner by candlelight and talk into the night.

Martin (*aside; to Susan*) I thought you weren't going to mention fire.

Susan I know . . . I know . . . but . . .

Anne We are not here for dinner. We cannot stay.

Erica We used to have dinner parties—when I was a girl. That's how I first met Sam, Hubert. Yes, he was definitely a Hubert at that dinner party ... he came with a girl ... now who was it? Why I believe it was Mavis Campion, she eventually married a bank clerk—and he committed suicide, so she wouldn't have done any better if she had married Hubert—she'd have lost him as well.

Martin Oh, Mother, really!

Erica I remember I wore a silver dress with a low cut back ... they were very fashionable, but I was the first person round here to dare to wear one ...

Anne Mother.

Erica Your grandmother wasn't very pleased—thought it was improper ...

Susan Mother!

Erica ... and your grandfather wasn't pleased about Hubert—said he was sly. I suppose he was ... sly ... yes, sly, simple Sam Strong.

Martin It's no good, she's rambling deliberately—let's go and see if there's anything left of the garden. Perhaps when we come back she will be more co-operative.

Anne Ever the optimist.

Ann, Susan and Martin exit

Erica And then there was the time ... where are you? Don't go. Don't leave me. Where are they? Have they gone?

The Man and the Woman move towards Erica from the shadows

Woman Have who gone?

Erica The children—have they gone?

Woman Yes, dear.

Erica Don't let them go. I want them. I don't want them to leave me.

Woman We are here.

Erica But my children ...

Woman They'll be back.

Erica They want me to go into a home. You know that don't you.

Man Well, they're only doing it for the best, you know.

Erica Best! How can they know what's best. They left me. They left me to live in this house all alone.

Woman Little birds must leave the nest you know.

Erica You never went into a home. You found a better way.

Man. . . er . . . well . . . yes, I suppose so.

Woman Why don't you lie down, dear. Have a little sleep. Don't forget Dr Blake said he would be calling later.

Erica Did he? How do you know? I don't remember.

Man Yes, he was here this morning. He had hoped some papers would have arrived from America. When they do, he'll come back . . . that's what he said.

Erica America? America? Someone was talking about America.

Man Dr Blake.

Erica No, no.

Man Yes, he did, this morning. Dr Blake.

Erica Oh do stop saying Dr Blake at me. You're such a boring man. Always were. I know, it was Susan. Susan's Ted . . . he ran off to America. Did you know that?

Woman We knew he was over there—I don't know if he ran off.

Erica Yes, ran off, just like Sam. You remember Sam don't you— Hubert you called him. You thought he was sly, didn't you.

Man Hubert? Sly? Not me, Erica.

Erica Not you? But I remember you—standing there—all starchy and stuffy.

Man No, definitely not me.

Erica But . . .

Woman Oh, really. Don't carry on so . . . if Erica remembers you I'm sure she is right.

Man Oh, but . . .

Erica rises from her chair

Woman Where are you off to now, dear?

Erica I'm not "off to" anywhere. I am just going to change for dinner. Just like we used to, don't you remember?

Man Remember, why no . . .

The Man is quelled by a look from the Woman

Woman Of course we do. But why change, you're not having a party.

Erica My family are here, that's party enough for me. (*She goes to the wardrobe, rummages about and brings out an old evening dress*) Do you remember this?

Woman Um . . . why yes, yes of course. You wore it when . . .

Erica When I accepted Sam. I'm going to change now.

Woman Do you want some help?
Erica Help? Help? How could you help?

Erica exits to the kitchen

Woman How indeed.
Man Why are you talking to her like that. She needs help.
Woman She is perfectly capable of changing her dress.
Man I didn't mean that—she shouldn't be here. You heard what the doctor said, and apparently her children as well.
Woman I know, but I see no point in upsetting her. We are here to keep her happy. Talk to her, listen to her and try to see she doesn't do something silly.
Man Well I regard changing into an evening dress in the middle of the day as pretty silly.
Woman She's quite right—you are stuffy.

Anne, Susan and Martin come back

Martin It's a shame really—all gone to rack and ruin. It used to be a lovely garden.
Susan Oh, Martin. It hasn't been a lovely garden for years.
Martin It was when we were children—before all the visitors.
Anne And before the dancer.
Susan Yes, when we used to come down for weekends and holidays—all of us.
Anne What do you think Mother's doing. Mother!
Erica (*off*) I'm in the kitchen dear, changing.
Anne Changing what?
Erica My dress.
Anne What for?
Erica Dinner.
Martin Oh Lord, what crackpot scheme is she up to now?
Erica (*off*) It's not crackpot, everyone always used to change for dinner. A very civilized habit.
Martin How is it she can be completely deaf to all your remarks when you are three inches away and yet hear you clear as a bell through brick walls.
Anne It's called tactics.
Susan She's right you know—don't you remember on those holidays, the grandparents always insisted we change for dinner.

Martin Yes, I do, I hated it. All togged up, I used to create like the dickens.

Anne Yes, you did, and got sent to bed without any dinner.

Martin Yes—it was called tactics. Mother always came upstairs with something. Couldn't bear to see her little boy starve.

Susan (*laughing*) Jammy little devil. Any rate I enjoyed it, dressing up.

Anne You know, somehow I feel we have their support too—the grandparents.

Susan I expect we would have. Very upright and sensible, grandfather was.

Martin I can't really remember him.

Susan Tall, dark and no sense of humour.

Anne But there is a certain feeling about this room—don't you feel it?

Susan Just memories, we are in the dining room you know.

Man She's been out there ages. It's ridiculous, her behaving like this. We should do something.

Woman What? There's nothing we need do—I am sure. I am sure as I can be that we have all the help we need.

Erica enters, now fully dressed for dinner

Susan Mother, you look lovely.

Woman I see it still fits, Erica.

Erica Of course it still fits. I look after my figure.

Anne You have indeed.

Man You must have been a beautiful girl, Erica.

Erica Don't you remember? Now go away, Im not going to listen to any more of your flattery.

Anne I don't believe that.

Martin You know Mother, I always thought Father married you for your money. But I was wrong, he was swept off his feet by the most beautiful girl in the county.

Erica Well, it certainly wasn't for my money, or if it was it must have come as a nasty shock.

Susan What must?

Erica That there wasn't any. Hadn't been any money for years— just a decaying house. I suppose you children were too young to notice but your grandparents only knew how to live in the grand style, they didn't know how to work, how to make money. So they just used up the capital they had inherited and when it was finished so were they. That was the end. They just gave up. Nothing else for them to do.

Martin I never realised.

Erica Did you Susan?

Susan Well yes, I did notice that there were fewer "things" about each time we came down. I don't remember them dying—they just faded out of my life.

There is a pause

Erica They killed themselves.

The Man moves in to Erica

Man Killed? What's this talk about killing.

Erica Oh, do stop fretting. You know what I'm talking about.

Susan I'm not fretting, but I am surprised. You kept it very well hidden.

Man You're not thinking of doing something silly.

Erica Of course not, I'm not a silly person.

Erica waves the Man back into the shadows

It all happened just after Sam left—it was quite a busy year.

Martin Busy! Behold the mistress of the understatement.

Anne But we came to live here after father left, and then there were the visitors.

Erica Yes. The house was all that there was and I reckoned it would last my life out so I told you that your grandparents had gone away and to make ends meet I took "paying guests", as they used to be called. With all the excitement of new surroundings and schools I think you just forgot about your grandparents.

Susan Yes, I think we did—oh, isn't that terrible.

Erica Nonsense. The young can't be bothered to hang on to the old. I don't expect your son to remember me Susan—why I can't even remember him.

Susan Mother!

Erica Oh, I can remember him—a happy baby, dark hair like his father. But I can't remember his name, or where he is.

Susan Bobby—and he's in America with Ted.

Erica Oh, my dear, I didn't realize Ted had taken him, I am so sorry.

Susan It's all right mother—it's all worked out fine.

Erica America. Everyone keeps talking about America today.

Anne Everyone?

Erica Who was it? Oh yes, Dr Blake. He's expecting some papers or letters from America and apparently he's coming back again. All this toing and froing—it confuses me. I don't understand half what the man's talking about or why he keeps bothering me. I hope he doesn't come back today, two visits on one day is two too many.

Susan It's Ted. Anne, Martin—it's Ted—he is doing something.

Martin What?

Susan I don't know—but it's Ted who's doing something about Mother.

Martin Good for him. I always liked Ted.

Susan And he liked—likes Mother.

Erica Well it's nice to see a few smiles at last, better than the gloomy faces you've been wearing all day. Now I think we ought to organize some dinner.

Anne We're not stopping for dinner, Mother. Unless of course you want to get something ready for Dr Blake.

Erica Certainly not. He's not coming back, and even if he does he's not getting anything from me. One track mind that man's got.

Anne One track?

Martin What track, Mother?

Erica I don't want to talk about it.

Martin He wants you to go into a home, doesn't he, Mother?

Erica Yes, he does.

Martin Tell us about it.

Erica There's nothing to tell—I'm not going.

Susan You must, you can't stay here, there's nothing here to stay for.

Erica Of course there is. There's my bits and pieces and . . . and . . .

Susan And?

Erica My shadows. . . .

Anne Mother!

Erica . . . and memories

Martin You can't live on memories.

Erica Or charity. I cannot and will not live on charity.
Susan It's not charity, Ted's paying. I know that's what it's all about—Ted is paying.
Erica Ted?
Susan My Ted, your son-in-law.
Erica I don't want Ted's money.
Susan Ted is family. He loves you, always has. I know if he'd realized what . . . what squalor you would have been living in, he would never have left. But . . . I imagine he just wanted to get away.
Erica Well, he can stay away.
Susan Don't be so ungrateful. He is trying to help you. Ted is family—he's the father of your grandson—he's the man I love, he's my Sam.

There is a pause

Anne I've been thinking, Mother. Where did you get your dress?
Erica Where? I can't remember where dear, I've had it years and years. Somebody's cast off I expect. Oh no, it's one of mine. I think I kept it because it's the dress I was wearing when your father proposed.
Anne No, I didn't mean that, I meant where in the house?
Erica In the house?
Susan Anne!
Martin Don't be a fool, Anne.
Anne Oh—sorry. I just wondered.
Martin There are some things best left alone.
Erica What are you all talking about?
Susan Don't worry, Mother, you know how those two always talked in riddles.
Erica Yes, yes, I suppose I do. But it's been such a long time since we were all together. Why the last time we were all here together was . . .
Susan (*hurriedly*) Where did father propose to you?
Erica Pardon?
Susan Father's proposal. Was it romantic? Beside the lake in the moonlight? Down on one knee swearing to be yours for ever, liar that he was.
Martin Steady Susan.
Erica (*laughing*) No. Nothing like that. There was very little

romance in your father. It was in this room. After dinner one evening. Your grandparents had gone into the drawing-room to set up the bridge table—your father hated bridge—he had to think too much. Just as I was going out of the door he grabbed my hand and said "I am not going to play another hand of that boring game unless you promise to marry me." So I accepted. It was the easiest way.

Anne I don't believe it. You wouldn't accept a man just because you wanted a fourth at bridge.

Erica No, dear—it just happened that way. I would have accepted Sam anywhere, any time. I think ... I think I would even have accepted him even if I had been able to look into the future.

There is a pause

Martin Well, that's love.

Erica You should know, Martin. You came rushing down to tell me you were going to marry the most marvellous girl in the world—Sheila, wasn't it—and I haven't seen her yet. When are you going to bring her down?

There is a pause

Martin That was a long time ago. Before ... a long time ago.

Erica You mean it's broken off?

Martin Yes, yes you could say that.

Erica Oh, I'm so sorry, you seemed so happy. And what about you, Anne—still the career woman? Are you a director of your firm yet?

Anne Er ... no—no, not yet.

Erica What's happened?

Woman Nothing Erica, nothing's happened.

Erica What are you hiding?

Susan We're not hiding anything.

Erica Yes, you are—you are all hiding something from me. It's a conspiracy.

Man Don't be silly Erica. Why should there be a conspiracy? We have nothing to hide. We are your friends.

Woman Friends—old friends.

Anne We are here, we wouldn't hide anything, we wouldn't hurt you.

Erica My dress, my dress, you asked about my dress?

Woman It's a beautiful dress.

Erica Yes. It was in one of the bedrooms. That was what you meant, was it, Anne?

Anne Yes.

Erica And the rest of your question?

Anne The rest?

Erica Yes—"why wasn't it burnt, Mother dear?" Because it was in a tin trunk. I should have told you about the trunk shouldn't I?

Susan It doesn't matter now.

Anne You remember.

Erica Of course I do. That's the last time where we were all here together. My, that was quite a night—the night of the fire. And here was our hero, Martin the hero. Everyone said so.

Martin Mother!

Susan It's true. You saved Mother.

Erica And then you went back for the girls. Martin, the hero, everyone said so.

Martin Forget it—it's all over.

Erica The fire chief said I had caused it with the gas ring. I did not. It was the wiring. The wiring is all gone to pot.

Martin Which is why you shouldn't be here now. There's no electricity at all—no gas—living by paraffin lamps. Cooking in squalor. It's crazy Mother, and it's sending you crazy too.

Erica Do you really think so? Do you really think I'm crazy?

Susan No, no of course we don't, it's just an expression. But it is dangerous and unhealthy for you to be here and it makes us all very unhappy.

Erica Unhappy? All of you?

Anne Yes—very.

Martin nods

Erica (*crying out*) But I don't want to go away. This is my home. I will be lonely in an institution.

Woman Dr Blake wouldn't put you in an institution. He's an old friend.

Erica I shall be lonely. I shan't know anyone. There won't be anyone to talk to.

Woman Yes, there will. Lots of people, kind people, people who care.

Erica My shadows care.
Susan Your shadows love you—but they cannot help you.

The front door bell rings

Man (*from the shadows*) That will be Dr Blake.

The Man exits

Erica starts to cry

Martin Don't cry, Mother—love is all around—don't cry.

Dr Blake enters, takes Erica by the hand, leads her to the settee and sits

Dr Blake Come along now, Erica, crying? This isn't like you.

The Woman comes forward from the shadows

Woman She's been rambling on quite a lot this afternoon, doctor, and getting quite upset. I wondered about giving her a sedative but you said just to watch.
Dr Blake That's right, nurse. I expect she's been talking to the children, that's what she does most of the time. Now Erica, I have some good news, are you listening to me?

Erica nods

You remember Ted? Susan's Ted.
Erica Yes, of course. We were talking about him this afternoon. He left her and went to America.
Dr Blake He went to America after the fire. After Susan died in the fire. Yes, he went away but he's coming back now because he wants to look after you.
Erica Me?
Dr Blake Yes. Now, he has asked me to get you into South Holt— it's a home for the retired, not a nursing home, not a lunatic asylum, nothing to worry about, a place where a number of pleasant, independent, elderly people are living.
Erica I don't want to go.
Dr Blake Don't be stubborn, Erica. Ted wants to help. Susan would have wanted him to.
Susan Please, Mother, please.
Dr Blake When I eventually managed to track him down I wrote

to him about you and asked him what he suggested. Well, we've had a lot of correspondence and he's coming back to England. If everything works out all right and he can find a house and a job he wants you to live with him and Bobby but, most of all, he wants you out of this ruin.

Erica It's my home.

Dr Blake We can come and get some of your special bits. But right now I have a car waiting. Come along.

Erica But my children . . . my shadows . . .

Dr Blake Leave them, Erica—let them go. Let them rest in peace now. Come with me.

Dr Blake goes to the door and waits. Erica rises but hesitates

Anne Go with him—we love you.

Martin Go—your "hero" begs it of you.

Erica moves to the door and turns as Susan speaks

Susan Mother . . . give my love to Ted and Bobby.

Erica nods. Susan, Anne and Martin move together as they watch her leave

Erica exits with Dr Blake

CURTAIN

FURNITURE AND PROPERTY LIST

On stage: Much furniture to suggest a cluttered room
Much dressing to indicate overcrowded surfaces
Chair
Settee
Wardrobe. *In it:* old evening dress
Table

Off stage: Cup of tea (**Erica**)

Personal: **Dr Blake:** doctor's bag

LIGHTING PLOT

A living room. No practical fittings required

To open: general lighting, not too bright, with edges of room in shadow

No cues

EFFECTS PLOT

Cue 1   **Susan:** "... they cannot help you."   (Page 17)
Front door bell rings

www.ingramcontent.com/pod-product-compliance
Ingram Content Group UK Ltd.
Pitfield, Milton Keynes, MK11 3LW, UK
UKHW021817150726
7214IPUK00017B/171